I0180614

little Girl of 3

Healing Journey of The Feminine Heart

Donna Mazza

Little Girl of 3

Copyright © 2018 by Donna Marie Mazza

Cover Created by: Yrvens J. of YJDesigns -
hello@yjdesigns.co

Printed by CreateSpace, an Amazon.com Company @
www.createspace.com

Interior Design: Beverly E. Barracks @
bebarracks@gmail.com

Graphic Image: Yrvens J. of YJDesigns -
hello@yjdesigns.co

Scripture quotations are from the ESV® Bible (The Holy Bible, English Standard Version®), copyright © 2001 by Crossway, a publishing ministry of Good News Publishers. Used by permission. All rights reserved.

Scripture taken from *The Message.* Copyright © 1993, 1994, 1995, 1996, 2000, 2001, 2002. Used by permission of NavPress Publishing Group.

Scripture quotations are taken from the Holy Bible, New Living Translation, copyright © 1996, 2004, 2007, 2013 by Tyndale House Foundation. Used by permission of Tyndale House Publishers, Inc., Carol Stream, Illinois 60188. All rights reserved.

All proprietary and legal privileges are the sole property of *Donna Marie Mazza,* the Author. Dissemination, storage, scanning or copying of this book is forbidden without written permission, other than for review purposes. You may contact the author at: littlegirlof3@gmail.com.

ISBN-13: 978-0692058602
ISBN-10: 0692058605

Printed in the United States of America

Dedication

I dedicate this Book to Jesus, as without Him I Am Nothing!

To my children: Cris, Gia and Nick.

You "3" saved me in more ways than you will ever know: You are my "3" heart-beats. ♡

Love, Mom

Foreword

"Numbing the pain for a while will make it worse when you finally feel it." - J.K. Rowling

Little Girl of 3 will take you on a journey of inner healing that many women often never get the chance, or take the time to do. We internalize our pain and continue with life while not dealing with the experiences we encountered that have somehow shaped the woman we are today. *Little Girl of 3* speaks to women in a way that only another woman would understand. In reading this book you will become privy to some of the struggles and pain the author has endured, but you will also get to see how she overcame those challenges as she shares some steps that have helped her.

On a personal note, as a young lady, wife, mother, and minister whose life is mostly in the lime light, it can be difficult to take time for yourself; but you too will be able to unwind and relate to *Little Girl of 3*. As you digest page after page, specifically Chapter 4 (for me), you'll begin to look within and discover that there are some experiences that you've also suppressed. One of my mottos growing up was *"if it isn't voiced it isn't real."* *Little Girl of 3* reminded me that I had lost my voice because I presumed the pain would eventually fade away; I was wrong. When we fail to confront childhood trauma, whether emotional or physical, one negative

Foreword

experience can trigger years of captivity. So, get ready to recapture the *Little Girl of 3* within, as it's sure to cause you to self-reflect and self-examine your beliefs and motives, while tugging on your emotions for change.

The author does an incredible job in opening the eyes, as well as the heart of her readers. She invites us to journey along with her while helping us to look deep within to reclaim our God given voice. She encourages us to empathize with those around us instead of judging one another. Her words take form of life and will liberate those who read it. Throughout the book she points us towards the one who has healed in every way, shape, and form; God, Himself. If you're ready to face your fears, confront your pain, and find your heart's inner healing, this book is a great start. *Little Girl of 3* is me; *Little Girl of 3,* she is you.

Tracy Simon, Prophet
Co-Pastor of Activation Church
West Palm Beach, FL.

Table of Contents

Introduction

Wherever the Lord finds a broken heart He fills the cracks with light and love. You know your heart is unchained when you can look back at your life's history and see it as a beautiful tapestry with all its imperfections that tell a story of courage, determination and love.

If you Sow seeds into a heart that needs healing, you will be successful. Sow in tears reap in joy; no matter how dark it gets; no matter how far you fall, you are never out of the fight to the top of the mountain. We must unpack our baggage for *forgiveness* to work.

> "If there's to be any resolution, I've got to peel my pride away; Just between you and me I've got something to say... Just between you and me Confession needs to be made, Recompense is my way to Freedom... Confession is the road to healing, forgiveness is the promised land... I'm longing to make amends...- Excerpts from DC TALK's song - 'Between you and Me.'"

You're not where you started, you are somewhere completely new every day; love what matters. See what's there, illusions make you unaware.

You need to know where someone has been before you know the essence of who they are.

Love is a movement;

Love is a revelation;

We feel what we believe;

> "No one ever made a difference by being like anyone else." - Barnum and Bailey Movie - 2017

A divine path within us is created, but we must listen to the voice within to find it. Rest and stepping back is so vitally important. It enables us to gain a new perspective, as we persevere and learn, we will see our individual tapestry at the end of the age.

And I heard the Lord say....

"You are schizophrenic with your words. You are blessing and cursing at the same time; you are making your angels schizophrenic; because you are sending them out and calling them back." I could see my angel standing tall, arms crossed while tapping his foot, looking down upon me and saying 'are you finished yet?'"

Many have been waiting a long time for some desires, and the Lord said, *"did you ever consider that you are the delay?"*

"Me, not me. Oh, my goodness. Everything else, but not me. Everyone else, but not me."

Introduction

And the Lord shook His head, as I began to consider my speech. And it hit me and without even knowing, I cursed my blessings. So, I asked the Lord to help me in this season of words. God knows us inside out, He knows when and how we will slip and struggle, but He's looking at our determination and our hearts' motivations.

Visually, I see the saints who are crawling through the dirt just to grab onto the hem of His robe, for we are in the Season of Words.

Know that I will fall forward because of my Faith, but you I fear, will fall flat on your face. You are mad at God, and you question why, but did it ever occur to you to look at your lies? However, there is Good News, Salvation is at hand through Repentance; it's a Free Gift and the Grace of God.

I pray for your soul...

Forever Eyes

When I look into your Eyes all I see are
the dark dark lies –
Lies that hurt
Lies that bind
Lies that changed the course of time
As time went by you justified the dark
dark lies behind your Eyes
You never realized the deepest pain and
convinced yourself it was all a game
My dad was kept away from me and for
that, there was no paternity
I was robbed so young of my heart's
desire to have the love of a father and
child
You tried to say it was a little white lie
that took away a Little Girls' why
You've never repented or apologized for
the lies you hid behind those Eyes
But in the end, the truth prevailed and
you couldn't hold on to the deceitful
grail!

The further away I get from the memory of you, the more peace I have, moment-by-moment, day-by-day until I am on the other side of it. I may never have human understanding or confirmation of what you were thinking, as you walked away without a word in such a hurtful and cowardly way. But, I know that when I see the tapestry of my life, as I enter Heaven, I will know the plan and the purpose God had for my life. I will know what adversity taught me, and I will see how I carried on with a pure loving and forgiving heart. I can only hope and pray that someday, you will be touched so profoundly by God, that your life will be changed for the better, that you'll stop running and hiding from your pain, and let someone love you again.

So, *Little Girl of 3,* who could she be? She could be you; she could be me.

I present this book to all the little girls inside of our hearts. The little girls who have gone

through the wilderness and survived or need wisdom and understanding on how to survive.

My hope is that the God inspired words on these pages will touch your little girl's heart, moving you forward in empowerment to tell your stories that will aid in unlocking the hearts of others. ♡

Chapter One
A Little Girl's Story

Awoman's voice is her most powerful tool in God's arsenal, and it's where we are attacked the most. It wasn't until I began writing this book that I was able to put the pieces of the puzzle together about the voice of the "*Little Girl of 3*."

I didn't see that this was where satan was attacking her since she was a child, using adults and the people who were supposed to love and protect her. Always professing *"seen, but not heard,"* using emotional and physical abuse to cause her to feel less than, and creating injury to her mouth that needed to be wired shut. If that's not a sign, I don't know what is!

The veil was thick over her eyes until the revelation of this assault was laid out in print and

it brought tears to that *Little Girl of 3* eyes. Awareness is the beginning to uncover the hidden so we can successfully go after it. I encourage you to journal daily your deepest feelings. Practice having conversations with God and you'll be amazed at what you see in print that you never saw before. Make no mistake, satan had a deep hatred for Eve and he continues to hate all women.

We must heal our wounds and we must audible speak out against evil. God can read our thoughts, but He tells us to speak to our mountains in belief and they will move. We can't just think it in our heads, we must verbalize aloud and keep verbalizing. When you feel a heaviness with speaking out loud or when wanting to pray that's an attack. Don't give up, call on that warrior spirit deep inside every woman. We must scream out, we must use our voices over our lives, our families and our

world. We are to be seen and heard and God has given each one of us boldness and grace.

This God given book is my prophetic voice and assignment to speak loud and clear to the nations, while putting satan on notice that women will not be stopped. They will arise a fresh, they will speak with a new boldness without fear, and they will conquer the demons all in the Name of Jesus. So, arise warrior princesses; the time to speak is here. ♡

Could it possibly be at 3, you could lose your will and become depressed, oppressed and your path becomes set for life?

During the period of time this *Little Girl of 3* grew up, she would often hear "children are seen, but not heard." Without any understanding of how to process this, she became fearful, quiet and shy. But on the inside, she was screaming—let me out, let my voice out, but the fear and anxiety overwhelmed her little heart.

She wanted to be relevant. She wanted to be loved. She wanted to be heard and cared for. She wanted to feel safe and protected; that *Little Girl of 3.*

In the summer of 1962, on a hot June night, she sat outside of the hospital with her grandparents awaiting the birth of her sister. As excited as she was, she could have never prepared for what happened. It would cut her little heart to pieces and would forever alter her life. She became a fatherless child; as he walked out of her life. She sat fatherless awaiting the birth of her sister; her path of feeling abandoned was set. Many believe that a child of 3 couldn't possible have the ability to experience or remember the deep feelings of rejection, so no care or acknowledgement was given to her little broken heart. At the time, she didn't know or understand what it all meant, she just knew how she felt; an empty hole in her heart. A hole that was never filled no matter what she

accomplished in her life, the ache of never experiencing the love of a father.

She grew up in a religious way, knowing of a God, but not as Daddy God. By not having a relationship with her biological father, even though she had many around her that loved her, this little girl was missing that key relationship in a little girls' heart; the love of her Daddy. Her heart was broken and no one knew, no one gave her heart the time of day. But God knew because from before the foundation of the world, this *Little Girl of 3*, was marked for His Kingdom. Now, the number 3 is the Fathers' number of the Trinity and even though she felt lost, she was predestined to be found by God the Father, Jesus her Savior, and the Holy Spirt, her comforter.

At the age of 6 (3 doubled), she had a memory of staying at the Jersey Shore for her summer vacations, in what was referred to as a rooming house. It was an old house with many

13

floors and rooms; the bathroom was shared and it had a large kitchen. The huge kitchen was where everyone who stayed there would congregate. This was a house filled with priest and nuns; a Holy house to her. She was joyful there and they became a special sort of family, as she felt relevant being in the midst of it all.

She watched and played, as they conversed and had socialized gatherings in the oversized kitchen. She was the only child amongst all the adults and because of this, she felt far older than her years; she felt like she belonged.

On one occasion, she was able to sleep on the sunporch; a glass room with white-half curtains. As the sun rose, a bright light came through the uncovered window tops, and she had a vision of doves, and a peace (*shalom*) came over her as she awoke. This was a happy place, but little did she know, it was God's Spirit watching over her.

During the 6th year of her life, tragedy struck her little heart again. Her beloved grandmother whom she affectionately called *Nana*, became ill and was hospitalized. Her *Nana* was in her fifties and of Italian decent. She suffered with diabetes and polio which caused her to have one leg shorter than the other. But, Nana didn't allow her disability to hinder her, she was strong willed and hearty. She was the pinnacle in teaching the *Little Girl of 3*, how to be a proper little girl and how to take care for her body, but most of all, how to continue to survive.

Though she never heard *Nana* complain about her conditions, and she was steadfast in all she did with beauty and grace, but even as a child, she could see the sadness behind her Nana's eyes; the burdens she bared. Could it be her voice was taken as well?

As she was sitting in the cold hospital in the hall outside of Nana's room, she could see her in the bed as the door opened and closed. Back

15

then, children were not allowed in the rooms. It was as though they were invisible and no attention was given to their feelings. Consequently, she never got to say one last goodbye or give her one last hug or say, "I love you," one last time.

The *Little Girl of 3* was frozen by fear. Why didn't she run into her room? Why didn't she disobey the rules? Suddenly, she was gone from her life like her dad, and no one paid attention to her, no one saw her heart and a little girl's loss.

Soon after, her mother remarried and she and her sister were moved from the City of Philadelphia away from her lifelong friends into the country. She was 9 (3 tripled), entering the 3rd grade, and the Trinity on many levels was with her, watching over her little life, but she didn't know it.

She had so much loss in the nine years she was on the earth, and from that point on, she

struggled with learning, had very few friends and felt like an outcast. She was teased and bullied and physically hit in school and at home. She was on a downward journey and for her age, it was more than she could bear, the loss of her dad, grandmother and the city she loved. All these circumstances created a deep, deep void of sadness, low self-worth, and anxiety mixed with great fear. No one knew, no one cared, and no one saw the heart of the *Little Girl of 3*.

Chapter Two
Marked

There was something inside her that made her press on through the loneliness and internal despair. She took on one challenge after another; accomplishing many things. She danced and swam and played sports. By the age of 16, she was winning awards on local, regional and state levels for fashion design and cooking. Basically, anything she touched she accomplished, and yet, nothing satisfied the huge hole in her heart.

It seemed she couldn't escape fear. It was at home, at church, in school and the ongoing message was 'you will never measure up, you will never be good enough, you have no voice!!!' We love you, but would constantly hear 'we don't like you,' was a regular household mantra. At this point in her life, she didn't realize God

marked her as His Chosen. God loves the least of these and she definitely was qualified. God implanted within her broken heart, the drive of a bulldozer. Every single time she was knocked down, her bulldozer spirit would lift her up stronger and more determined than ever.

She often thought she was a survivor which in many respects was true, but the greater truth; she was more than a conqueror and adversity was her teacher. Without it, she couldn't have learned, blossomed and overcame. God's Spirit inside her caused her to press forward on the journey of her *little girl's heart*. She went through school very much feeling like the *ugly duckling* and in many cases, a wall flower, basically blending in and always feeling less than everyone else.

Until that one day, in her senior year, when she was involved in a school accident and became infamous. Sitting in gym class, her female gym teacher lost her cool, as a male

student entered the gym. She hurled a tennis racket across the room at him, and it hit the floor and bounced up into the mouth of the *Little Girl of 3.* The racket shattered and knocked out her teeth, which caused her much pain, bruising and eventually wiring her jaw. She needed so much dental work that it took months-and-months to reconstruct and restore the damage.

Because of this accident, she became the school *pariah;* an outsider. Every girl in that gym became a witness in the law suit which was inevitable, no one spoke to her as she would walk the halls, sadly, no one saw her *little girl's heart.*

A year that was to be the best, was the worst nightmare, and to add insult to injury, to her already low self-worth. She didn't realize that many attacks on her life were against her voice in order to silence this *Little Girl of 3.* She must have had something important to say, for satan

to take such an assault against her voice after all, she was a child; it almost worked, but God intervened.

Chapter Three
Womanhood

As she grew into womanhood, she carried the *Little Girl of 3* deep inside her soul. She looked for love in all the wrong people which only amassed more hurt, more lies, and more worthless feelings. Going after people who would eventually leave her and creating a self-fulfilling prophecy of not being good enough, pretty enough or smart enough. Time-and-time again, she would pick herself up, but only to return to the same scenario; broken hearted. The Bible says it this way:

"Like a dog that returns to his vomit is a fool who repeats his folly." Proverbs 26:11

23

It was like watching a boxing match when you are SCREAMING "don't get up, don't get up;" and they get up for more. With each new punch, it took a bit more away from her soul.

In her early twenties, she was about to be married because it seemed to her that the only way out of an unhappy home life, was to marry. As she was gathering the documents for the church and State to marry, a deep shattering secret was uncovered in her life.

When her mother remarried, the *Little Girl of 3* was told yet another lie, which she believed most of her life, that her stepfather had adopted her. As far as she knew; he was her dad. She never had any reason to question what she knew to be, until that day. She was 21 (7 times 3), and was surprisingly informed by the State, that her name and all her documents were forged, and if she planned on marrying, she would have had to use her birth name. Unfortunately for that *Little Girl of 3*, she had never been adopted.

Once again, she felt worthless, discarded, betrayed. Who was she now? That *Little Girl of 3* with no identity, suddenly heard a distinct voice tell her "it is time for you to get away from your family or you will become just like them."

Embroiled in lies and abuse at the time, she had no idea who was speaking to her, but intuitively, she knew she had to go. Deep inside of her, what she thought was true love sadly wasn't. Though she loved him, it was an escape from the life she had; once again, her survival instinct kicked in. She moved 2,500 miles away and severed all ties with her family for the next 37 years.

They began their life and had 3 children that she adored by the time she was 29; she worked hard to be a good wife and mother to her family. At thirty, she was left with three children, no money, no career and standing in the food stamp line. Her husband bankrupted them and left her with the kids for someone else; what a

blow, yet again. With no time to think or wallow or process the hurt and betrayal, that bulldozer strength rose up inside her as she picked up the pieces of her life now with three children and entered cosmetology school, which birthed a passion inside of her for a career she was good at.

She remarried in her thirties. There was a part of her that married for survival and help with her children. She lived a monetarily successful life raising her children and working in a career she never dreamed of having. It showed her that out of adversity and turmoil, good can come, but still, the emptiness was always there.

She became so successful that she opened her own business and worked hard at it from the ground up, but in the midst of what she thought was success, once again, she discovered lies and rumors of cheating from her then husband. How could this be? Having been down that

road before with no time to think or process the events, the bulldozer spirit came out and scooped her up and thus, she moved on.

Now in her mid-forties and running a business, she married husband number three. Needless to say, this marriage was filled with the same betrayal and lies. This time, she lost everything; marriage, business and home.

Her bulldozer spirit didn't come out and her survival tactics didn't kick in. She was exhausted and broken beyond broken. Sobbing with heart wrenching pain, she stopped running and started what was to be the most glorious adventure of her life, but she didn't yet know it.

God showed up in her life, in the midst of chaos, confusion, homelessness and grief. She finally heard her Father's Voice, and ran into His Spiritual arms. And in September of 2008, in her Jubilee Year, she was Saved for Eternity and now the real work began.

Chapter Four
She Is Me

That *Little Girl of 3* is me and in many cases; you. We are the divine beauties and in the end, we came through it all by looking up.♡

The journey of our hearts is ingrained in our DNA. It's our longing pursuit to get back to Eden. For many, the journey is to find peace, salvation, healing and worth in themselves, and in knowing a Father who will *never leave or forsake them.*

"As God has brought us into His kingdom, He has promised that He will never leave us nor forsake us."
Heb. 13:5

I now understand the significance of the 3 in my life, it was my road map leading me to my Eden. That *Little Girl of 3* inside me was my guardian angel, helping to guide me to my Fathers' Heart, as I became reborn into my true family; God the Father, the Son, and the Holy Spirit.

It has now become my greatest commission on this earth TO SPEAK the words that reach, teach, and touch the hearts of women on a God ordained healing path, orchestrated by the *Little Girl of 3.*

You will be the beauty in the end. You can come through anything if you look upward and not back, if you are walking forward, but looking backward, you will trip. So, look pass your past and keep your eyes on Jesus.

"When you stand guard at the heart of your mind, you will become aware of roots that are holding you captive from your destiny." - Donna Mazza

30

Chapter Five
Broken-Hearted

How can we genuinely love others, if we ourselves are broken-hearted? Most often, we look for people, places and things to fill the void within us, hoping to be satisfied. Hoping to be revived, and not feel the pains of our emotional traumas sustained in what we call life.

But, is there another way; another life we could be living? It seems so simple that the key to loving others would be for us to first be healed. It's the hardest journey we could ever embark on, but the most rewarding and healing we will ever know, but we must involve our Creator. It will cause us to dig deep into our past hurts and fears, contend with our shame,

31

abandonment, addiction to drugs, alcohol and even people.

God created each of us with a void within our hearts and the only thing that will fill that void and turn on the light in our lives, and heal our broken hearts, is God; the missing void is God.

It places us in an environment of vulnerability and dependence that many do not want to address, so they continue to carry around the chains they have amassed all their lives until death or surrender. Which will it be? For me, I chose to die to myself interest and willingly surrendered to God's free invitation to fill the empty void, after a lifetime of running in the wilderness.

This was my second chance to live and have the freedom my heart has always longed for; you can have it too. I saw that all my self-repair, striving, and replacing my hurt with people and things was inadequate and had no lasting value.

Life was a rollercoaster, devoid of peace and true meaning.

I realized that on this journey involving the heart, I didn't know what true love was. All around us through the media and entertainment, we are told love is romantic feelings. We are bombarded by sex in movies, TV shows, magazines and the sheer culture of the times we are now living in. Why? Because love and sex sells, thus bringing in big money while depleting and downright cheating people out of the essence of true love; Godly Agape Love.

Deep abiding Agape Love is kind and generous, peaceful, patient, full of joy and forbearance for one another and it is communicative and understanding. But, we can only love to the capacity that our hearts are healed. Christ has taught us through His words all things. We just need to open our spiritual eyes and apply the manual.

Often in our humanity, we try to be judge and jury where others are concerned; that position belongs solely to God. Loving people doesn't mean we must surround ourselves with those who are not on the same journey or purpose, it simply means be kind, show goodness, don't gossip, don't judge, but instead, pray for God's Will to be done in all matters.

We are to work on our own personal healing and excellence and not be looking left and right for someone to blame. So many times, we try to interject our will into situations which solves nothing and works to control others. Much of what we are experiencing in these times is a me centered society, when all along God's desire is to unify us together for the greater good of people on earth and the only way to this is to be healed.

We must see all people as having worth as God sees them. As I embarked on my journey, I had to see God as my Father which for me, as

a child abandoned by her father, it was very difficult. Like many, I didn't understand what that meant so, this was the first layer to peel off my heart. Ouch!

Many suffer from abandonment not feeling wanted or loved by the most significant of relationships and in my *Little Girl of 3* heart, I became broken, feeling abandoned, sad and second-best. The first step on the journey was to surrender to God and make Jesus my Lord and Savior, but until that step was taken He could not teach and I could not hear.

Chapter Six
Returning to Virgin Hearts

How do we get the virginity of our hearts back? How do we get the purity back? How do we get our life's blood pumping through every fiber of our bodies? How do we become new in the old?

It only happens through Jesus Christ. If you have read anything so far in this book that has touched your heart, brought a tear to your eyes or made you question yourself, then perhaps you are ready for the surrendering step in your life to be reborn into the new. Say this simple prayer:

Father, I am done running. I am done hiding. I am ready to submit my life to you through your

Son, Jesus Christ. I ask you to open my heart, change me, heal me, rearrange me for your Kingdom purpose for my life. In Jesus Name, Amen.

Now, Let's Begin!

Even when we feel we are heart healed, life happens and it shows us our journey is not complete until the end of the age. Things will come up, things will go wrong, we will get hurt and be sad. We will experience every emotion possible because of our humanity, but when we have something bigger than ourselves on the inside, we are never alone. We can call upon the inner strength to see us through. Is it easy? No, but we can conquer all things with God.

Our minds can defeat us, our thoughts can destroy our spirit, we have fallen to such deceptions, of a generation of people never claiming any responsibility for their pain and living in a grey area of one foot in and one foot out. Clearly, we must be ever so careful of what

we think *"as a man's thoughts go so does he."* Our thoughts, our mindsets, are one key to how our circumstances will turn out to simplify it, bad thoughts, bad direction, good thoughts, good direction.

What we allow into our mind and what we speak can make all the difference between success and failure. The only place the devil can speak to us is in our mind and its where he tries to control us. We are battling a sinister force, a liar and deceiver that wants to see us depressed, oppressed, sad, addicted and utterly destroyed.

If we can grasp the concept that our mind is in a battle, then it puts all things into perspective. Who do we want to win this battle? It doesn't mean we ignore the emotions or the situations that arise. It simply means, we need to recognize the feelings that the situations evoked in us and work through those feelings and emotions for a positive healthy outcome.

An amazing word I discovered is NEVERTHELESS. It speaks such truth and when used, it reaffirms our steadfast belief in our healing. God doesn't expect us to immediately have all things worked out, but nevertheless, He is looking for our partnership to continue our growth on our journeys.

When we stuff our feelings and emotions, we allow ourselves to close down our hearts. We put up unhealthy barriers and walls, which leaves us chained in bondage. The goal was always to go back to the root, back to the beginning until we get on the other side of it. When God parted the Red Sea, the people walked to the other side to start a new free life. We are much the same, we must go through it with courage and believe in our freedom to get to the other side of it. Are you tired of revisiting the same mountain, the same places, the same situations, over and over?

Happiness of the heart is attainable. Here are some of the key steps on your journey:

1. Learning to forgive self and others;
2. Accepting responsibility for our part in things and repenting;
3. Confessing our wrong doings;
4. Learning to break soul ties;
5. Learning about spiritual warfare, witchcraft and curses;
6. Learning healthy boundaries; and
7. Learning how to care for your body and your health.

As we move forward I will outline the journey God showed me for success. And my prayer is that it blesses you with peace, joy and freedom. Our journeys are personal, but many of us experience the same thread of hurt and brokenness. I walked this out over the past nine years; step-by-step; God walked with me. He held my hand; He dried my tears and at times, He carried me, but most of all, He loved me through it. I believe that as we work on our

hearts' condition, we will begin to hear God's Voice more clearly concerning our journeys.

We can certainly understand on some level that brokenness comes from brokenness. But, what about those who were born into an ideal loving family, with no abuse, parents' marriage intact, with God centered homes and yet, they too have brokenness?

God revealed to me that He has a plan and purpose for every individual on this earth, if we will submit and in getting us to do so, He teaches us in a way that is completely individual and tailor made for us. This is why we should never judge where someone is at in their process because we simply don't know God's ultimate plan for them.

The wilderness is where our attention is captured so, we are not prisoners of our past instead, we are forging ahead as conquerors of our future. I believe we are in the dispensation of time where God is raising up warriors who

are healed, unchained and healthy, in order to move forward in battle for the Kingdom on Earth.

Chapter Seven
Miracles

T he best way for God to get our attention is to show His sovereignty through Miracles. Early in my journey, I diligently began studying God's word, taking classes and going to church, as there was much I didn't understand, but I stayed the course and pressed in.

This was a time period when I had nothing, no possessions, no home, and I landed on the doorsteps of my sons' one-bedroom apartment and he took me in and for eight months, we shared the space.

Even though my life was turned upside down, God made sure I was able to run my private suite salon, but all else was removed so that all my attention was focused on Him.

As I sat on my bed studying one day, I had the TV tuned into *"Sid Roth, It's Supernatural"* and his guest was *Dr. Gary Wood.* As I studied and listened to *Dr. Wood,* he called out *"someone with a rotator cup problem will be healed now"* and suddenly, tears flowed down my face— *"I had been experiencing severe shoulder pain, and as a hair stylist, this could have been devastating, but God stepped in and supernaturally healed me."* My shoulder was set on fire with an intense heat and the pain never returned; I was ecstatic. This was my first healing Miracle.

During this time, my son was going through a very difficult period emotionally, and he was deeply depressed. As I awoke one morning to get ready for work, I heard an audible Voice that said *"take the guns."* You can imagine my surprise, I had never heard God's Voice. As I entered the closet, I saw the guns in their cases and I said *"Oh no, he wouldn't hurt himself."* Then I heard the Voice booming "TAKE THE

GUNS." This time I didn't argue, I moved quickly and took the guns. God said, *"take the guns, but leave the cases and put them in your purse and go to work."*

Later that day, my son texted me and said, *"that was a good idea you took the guns, mom."* The only way he would have known that the guns were gone was that he opened the cases in an attempt to take them out. God knew every action, every step, and to prove it to me, He saved my son from a tragic end and orchestrated every move.

Now, in the wilderness of losing everything, God proved that He was with me and my family. So, in that small one-bedroom shared apartment, I found two amazing life altering Miracles and I learned in the nothingness, I had everything that mattered.

The next time I heard God's audible Voice was when He wanted me to part with the only

possession of value I had left. It was a diamond Bezel Rolex watch that I loved. My watch started to slow down and I heard God say, "I want you to sell it" so, I went over to Palm Beach Florida to a small jewelry shop and got a quote, but left with the watch. Though I was new at hearing God's Voice, I was still disobedient. With the watch still in my possession after 6 months, I heard God's Voice again saying *"sell the watch or I will see to it that it has no value."* Frantically, I high tailed it over to the jewelry store and told them I was ready to sell!

Six months prior, the store had hand written their offer on a receipt, as they still operated in a very old-fashioned way. Luckily for me, they had pinned the offer to a corkboard in their backroom; that in itself was amazing. I immediately took the watch off and said,

"Take it, I'm ready to sell!!"

Once I obeyed, and the watch was no longer in my possession, the Peace of God came over me like a blanket; a Peace that could have only come from above. As promised, a week later I received a check in the mail for the sale of the watch which was the exact amount I needed to cover the taxes I owed.

God is looking for our obedience and if we are willing to part with anything He asks of us, He will see that we are Rewarded. I was starting to realize the importance of Trust and Obedience and God's faithfulness to speak to me in a tailor made personal way.

As my journey progressed, I was introduced to the ministry of the Holy Spirit and many of the greats like Kathryn Kuhlman, Benny Hinn, Heidi Baker, Dr. Randy Clark, just to name a few. I became fascinated with this interactive ministry. It gripped my heart and I was on my way into the Holy supernatural world of deliverance. I knew that if you wanted

something bad enough, you needed to press in and take action.

My desire at this time was to see angels and develop my heavenly language. So, I began praying and asking God for the gift and I was led to a small book called *"Good Morning Holy Spirit."* As I read this book, I believed with my whole heart every word, and every experience Benny Hinn had as a young boy.

After finishing the book, I continued to pray to see angels and to my delight, one morning as I was getting out of bed, I found a pure white feather by my feet. I knew my angel had visited me. There was no doubt in my mind, since I owned nothing feather filled on my bed. This was the only explanation plausible. I was learning that God heard the desires of my heart and my faith was growing.

Shortly after I awoke one Sunday, I sensed in my spirit the name of a church I had never attended, it was only 25 minutes from my house.

As I got ready for the day, the Lord told me to go to this church. I didn't need to be told twice, so I looked it up and I was off on this adventure because with God, our daily walk is always an adventure.

As the service began, I felt an excitement in my spirit and my senses were on high alert wondering what God was up to. As the service neared its end, the Lord said, *"I want you to go up for prayer at the altar"* and He directed me to the woman He wanted to pray for me. As we joined hands, she began praying and suddenly, I realized I was praying in sync with her in a language I never heard or spoke before. With tears streaming down my face, overwhelmed with God's love for me, I felt such a sense of peace. It was a glorious, beautiful experience and I lost track of time as I was caught up in another realm.

This was God's gift of the Baptism in the Holy Spirit. Each step of my journey, God was

teaching me His lessons. When we have a desire in our hearts that aligns with God's plan and purpose, it will come to pass; only Believe.

In my process, I developed a love for journaling and was rarely without my tablet. As my relationship grew with the Lord, I would ask Him questions and eventually would realize that in the words I wrote, He was speaking to me. All my life I longed for a relationship with the Father I never had. I desired to be cherished as Daddy's little girl and there was still a part of my heart that felt fatherless.

God in His infinite wisdom knew all of my desires and one day as I was writing, He spelled out the new name He gave me 'SARI.' I thought it was a beautiful name and I loved it, but there was so much more to those four little letters. It was my new identify from my Father who cherished and adored me as His Beloved daughter. Such a small word with a life changing Hebrew meaning. No longer was I a fatherless

child and these are the words my Daddy God spoke:

"Sari, you will be lovely into old age with a grace to teach others about me. You are my faithful princess and I adore you. You my daughter are beautiful, strong and determined. You are from an important regal lineage and you are destined to bring kings to their knees as a spiritual seed planter and married wife."

Wow, this is how my Father sees me, the *Little Girl of 3.* And believe me, He has a new name and identity for each of you. All you need is to Believe.♡

As I became more aware of this new exciting Holy Spirit ministry, I went back to the religion I grew up in. I heard of a healing Priest coming to St. Ann's Catholic Church in West Palm Beach, Florida, and I was fascinated. In all my Catholic upbringing and schooling, I never once heard of any Priest doing this.

As I sat in the familiar pews reciting the ritual prayers, I sensed something very different. There were many in this service with sicknesses and in wheelchairs looking for a touch, for healing, and I thought to myself, there is nothing wrong with me so, what would I ask for?

As the Priest walked down the center isle he was calling out different people from the pews and as he made his way closer to me, he asked if there was anyone else that needed prayer and suddenly I jumped in front of him not even realizing what I was doing, and I asked him for healing of my broken heart. He paused for a moment and prayed beautiful words over my heart and instantly, I knew that my heart would be healed and my journey was set. The secret to my Miracle was; I Believed. God was building my faith one brick, one experience at a time and He was leading me on this journey of the heart.

As my hunger for more of God deepened and my understanding of the Holy Spirit

increased, I wanted to experience the Power that I was hearing about. So, I would visit churches and attend conferences and watch in amazement and awe, as people were being touched, fall to the floor shaking and convulsing; well at least that's what I thought at the time.

In my early journey, I didn't know what to make of it, but my inquisitiveness helped me press on. I was attending a conference in Orlando, Florida, with others from the small ministry I was in and one of the speakers was *Dr. Randy Clarke* from Bethel Church in California.

As we stood with our hands raised in prayer, Dr. Clarke said he wanted everyone to come up that felt an unction in their hearts and needed a touch from the Lord. All of a sudden, tears started to stream down my face, and from that day on, that's my signal that the Holy Spirit has come upon me.

As I made my way to the front, I knew deeply in my heart, that I desired a touch from the Lord, and I knew this was my time that He prepared. Yet, to be honest, I was fearful of the unknown of falling to the floor or what if nothing happened in front of all the people? As I tried to quiet myself, my mind was racing with thoughts of "what if I fell, would anyone catch me or would I get hurt?

I was in the second row from the stage along with many others. With my eyes tightly closed and my hands raised high, I could hear where Dr. Clarke was as he moved along the stage reaching down and touching each person that was closest to him. I kept my eyes closed as if afraid to open them and then it happened, as he touched the man in front of me, suddenly, in a split second, I felt a surge of *great power* hit me like a lightning bolt going through my heart and with a gust of wind, as if, I flew through the air and landed on the floor.

As I laid on the floor, tears streaming down my ace, I tried to process what just took place. Then, I heard God say in a joyful, playful manner, *"See, you didn't get hurt, and there were no spotters."* Then I remembered my angels and the sudden gust of wind, I knew they caught me and laid me on the floor. Father always knows best and He knew that He had to surprise me in order to take away my fear. I have always been a hands-on-tactical learner. I have to be touching, sensing, creating and experiencing to learn and this experience was tailor made for me. God knows each of us personally and if you become aware and in tuned with the Holy Spirit, you too will see and experience things out of the uniqueness of how God created you. I promise, this isn't just for me; it's for you too!

Along this journey, I have had a couple of pinnacle mentors and on one particular evening, March 27, 2015, I received a prophetic word from a well-respected prophet who was

my spiritual father. He said, *"you are going to be sliced with a knife and something will be implanted within and it is going to hurt, but the Glory that will come from it will be amazing."*

As I walked back to my seat, I said to myself, *"Oh, I don't like that word, can I have another?"* I had no idea what it meant and I put it out of my mind until June 28, 2015, exactly 3 months to the day (there's that 3 yet, again.) I was in church that morning, feeling a little under the weather and I was thinking I possible might have a stomach flu, but nothing serious.

Then, I heard the Lord say, "go up for prayer after church" and as we held hands, a forceful wind came at my stomach from the direction of the altar and the Holy Spirit whispered in my ear "go to the hospital." The hospital was right down the road and I drove there immediately and went to emergency. I told them I was ill, but I didn't know what was wrong because I had very few symptoms. After

a few tests, I was informed my appendix was leaking and they didn't know for how long, but my body was being poisoned and part of my colon tissue was being killed. I couldn't believe I was that ill with virtually no symptoms; I believe that was God's protection over me.

I was rushed into surgery at the hospital where my best friend was CFO; what a blessing. She lined up all the doctors and the surgeons and put me in under VIP status. If you have to be in the hospital that's the way to go.

The surgery went well, but satan and death had me in their sights. Over the next three months, I was hospitalized a total of four times. I became deathly ill with a life-threatening case of *c-diff,* a super-bug bacteria that only reacts to two medications; one I was allergic to and the other wasn't covered under my insurance plan. I was on a total of 16 weeks of a strong antibiotic and even after I was released, my body was not quite right.

During the time in the hospital all I could say was the Name of Jesus. I couldn't pray or read as I had absolutely no strength and my mind was full of medications. I remember this one particular time during my third hospital stay, laying in my room alone. All the blinds were closed and I yelled out *"Lord you can take me home I'm ready. I've had a good life, but if you choose not to take me then you need to heal me because I am not one to stay in this limbo."* I remember speaking it audible with force, I sensed I was mad and shortly after that, I began to improve.

But, I returned back to hospital one last time because I developed a cyst in my side from the poison in my body, but fortunately, this time around, the medications worked and by October, 2015, I was given a clean bill of health.

My medical bills were a whopping $250,000, and although I had insurance, my girlfriend wiped out all of my medical expenses. God

surrounded me with people who looked after me and cared for me. That season of my life was the hardest fight I had ever endured for my physical life. I could feel the fight in the spirit world over me like a tug-of-war.

Now that I was out of the hospital, it was time to rebuild my physical body; regain my strength while exercising my lungs and then the Holy Spirit guided me down the road of healing using specific foods, probiotic herbs, essential oils, essential nutrients from clay soil; potassium, calcium and magnesium, and raw D3, B vitamins and aloe.

God taught me about 'Gut Health' (foods with probiotics and alkalizing your system.) He led me to learn about organic non-GMO "genetically modified organisms"[1] free of processing antibiotics and hormones and His

---

[1] According to the World Health Organization, "Genetically modified organisms (GMOs) can be defined as organisms (i.e. plants, animals or microorganisms) in which the genetic material (DNA) has been altered in a way that does not occur naturally by mating and/or natural recombination.

leading sent me to watch a nine-part series of *"The Truth Project about Cancer."*

I began to implement all I learned and I added juicing to my daily routine. Within exactly one year from my ordeal on June 28, 2016, I was back to feeling normal. So many miracles on this journey and true to God's words, it would slice me and it would hurt, but it would be amazing and it was. To this day, I'm healthy, back at the gym and I continue to live an organic GMO free, grain fed, hormone free, and antibiotic free life.

During this season of my life, it became very clear to me that God wants us to be aware of our bodies (temples) and our health. He wants us to be educated about our bodies and not be led down the road of the spirit of Pharmacia. Far too many of His people are being medicated and taking drugs, they don't need, and getting treatments that are killing them. God created doctors, but we need to be aware that God is the

Supreme Healer, not man and we must listen to His Voice, and when we do, He will lead us.

I could not have lived without the wonderful surgeons who treated me, but God was the one that ultimately healed me and changed my life from that point on. Now, I will share with anyone who will listen to my healing testimony. Healing isn't just for me, it's for all to grab onto, as it's one of God's promises to us; so, start proclaiming your Healing Today!

Chapter Eight
Steps To Inner Healing

Repentance is at the root of all things that need change in our lives. To repent, we must become aware that something is not quite right within us. When we are operating solely in our flesh, we have no ability with any lasting effect to make this happen. True repentance always begins in the essence of God's whispers.

Repenting is a turning away, and that comes from a revelatory place deep inside of ourselves. It was never meant as a religious or condemning shameful act. It's simply an awareness of the new that God wants us to embrace. There are many times we get nudges that we ignore and consequently throw the keys away that will unlock our freedom. God wants to restore us!

What is it that keeps coming up in your heart and in your life, that God wants you to take a deeper look at...?

Growing up as a devout Catholic, we had to make weekly confessions to a priest in a dark box which were fear driven and condemning. My confessions were all about the bad and wickedness in me.

As God transformed my heart, I realized that confession is something that was meant to be a conversation of an awareness of our hearts' condition. It's a deep honesty about who we are in Christ and renouncing all the lies we speak or are spoken over us.

Confession is meant to set us free and align us with God's heart. What is it that you are wrongly believing about yourself or a circum-stance in your life concerning faults, mistakes, failures and sin that is keeping you from being set-free...?

Forgiveness is essential to our freedom and one of the most challenging actions to accomplish; though it is mandatory.

It requires us to let go emotionally and to attain peace of mind and in our hearts. It's not something you wish away and even when you believe you have forgiven or even forgotten, on the road of life, something may suddenly resurface. God is so amazing in His plan of Redemption for man, that He made provision in His word by telling us that we need to forgive seventy times seven. *Matthew 18:22* – *"Jesus saith unto him, I say not unto thee, Until seven times: but, Until seventy times seven.*

First Step:

We must become keenly aware of all of our feelings, emotions and thoughts about the situation and the people involved.

Second Step:

What do we believe the person owes us? What is our perception of what occurred? Basically, we need to step back and view the situation from another clear vantage point without all the emotions. Knowingly, it's not bad or evil to have thoughts of dislike, anger, even hate when you're trying to work through something. The problem lies in carrying that longer than you should and having it spill over into other areas of your life. For me, writing everything down step-by-step has been a powerful tool and at times when I'm finished, I am able to forgive and discard the papers saying it's finished.

Third Step:

Jesus has to be in this with you in order to release the person from the debt of unforgiveness. And, until we are able to rid ourselves of our inner feelings, forgiveness is not complete. It doesn't always happen immediately and even when you believe you have released

68

someone, down the road, something may arise from within that needs to be addressed at the root. This is a worthwhile process which can only be attained with the Lord and a willing heart.

In my life, I have noticed that once I became accustomed to the process and began cleaning out my heart from all past pain, hurt and disappointments of life, it was easier to forgive and thus the process became automatic. Knowing that I had a voice and a choice on what I would receive into my heart, I was no longer a target and I could stop hurtful words from taking root in my heart. I was no longer a victim and was less likely to allow things to slip into offense.

Fourth Step:

When you are ready to truly let go, ask Jesus to take it from you and when you have peace and rest in your mind and emotions, then it is finished.

I say this prayer:

"Father, I release ... to you for your divine wisdom, your will and judgment in this situation. I ask for your peace and protection to surround my heart as I release all my hurt and angry feelings and any debt I'm holding onto and I forgive and bless ..."

Fifth Step:

Please understand that not all people are meant to surround us. Neither, not all people are on the same journey, so forgiveness is one aspect and reconciliation is another. In order to reconcile, both parties must hear the call and have the desire to work through the steps to rebuild a stronger more trusting relationship.

Jesus showed us by examples that He was surrounded by multitudes, but not everyone was in His inner circle. So, we must heed His example and release those with blessings and move forward.

Soul Ties:

This is an extremely important area to our deliverance, freedom and healing for our lives. We all have souls that can be compromised through combining ourselves emotionally and physically with another person.

We are linked with others through marriage, friendships, our children, employers, clergy which can either be positive or negative depending upon the activities one is engaged in.

It's very important to know who we are surrounding ourselves with and what is being spoken over us by self and others. Word curses are very powerful and can set our course for negative thinking and performance. For me, I carried much of what was spoken over me as a child into adulthood and I had to break all those word curses out of my spirit in order to move forward. Some of what we tell ourselves, curses our own lives, as well. Any untrue negative speech can be a curse because it's contrary to

the way God made us and the way He sees us. The first soul tie we should cultivate is with God; the Father, Jesus and the Holy Spirit.

Negative soul ties evoke uneasy feelings which are big red flags that should not be ignored. They usually come with manipulation, lies, control, abuse, codependency sexual immorality. One way to test if you are questioning unhealthy soul ties in the present or from the past is to ask yourself the following:

1. Do I feel inferior; not good enough?
2. Am I trying to fix them?
3. Am I doing things I know are wrong, but to please them I do them anyway, creating shame and guilt?
4. Am I obsessive in my thinking; lustful thinking?
5. Have I engaged in any type of sexual act outside of marriage; or witchcraft?

Listed are some examples of witchcraft that society has made common place and could be open doors to demonic spirits if believed and are practiced:

Horoscopes, palm reading, hypnosis, channeling spirits, séances, Reiki, therapeutic touch, Ouija board, consult a medium, tarot cards, fortune-telling, horror movies, casting spells, good luck charms, psychic phenomenon, and crystal balls.

Many of us are taught about God, but not satan. As I began to embrace the whole idea that satan and his demons were real, I sat again and journaled all the things that I recognized as negative patterns in my life.

I wrote down all the word curses from self and others and I listed those names with whom I had sexual immorality and I also listed all demonic activity I encountered through movies, new age thinking, fortune tellers, horoscopes,

etc. And with each entry, I felt a falling off of burdens as though I was being unchained one-by-one-by-one.

Now, don't get me wrong, in the beginning it was a process and I had to have my belief systems in line with God so, I studied many writings about deliverance beforehand. I'm here to tell you first hand; it's attainable, but if you need assistance, seek out a deliverance ministry for guidance.

I had to recognize the evil;

I had to confess what I did;

I had to ask for God's forgiveness as well as forgive myself; and

I had to ask the Holy Spirit to take this from me, close the doors I opened, and to heal my heart.

Now, if those feelings or thoughts resurfaced then you must go deeper to dig up all of the roots. I believe that as we take this journey it will get easier to recognize the demonic, recognize those who are not good for us and eliminate

things quicker from our lives before they take root. The devil will always be there to lie, misdirect and shame us, but with healed hearts, we can ward off his attempts. Remember, each test and trial we endure, will help to mature us so, we cannot get discouraged; keep moving forward. ♡

Boundaries:

When dealing with feelings of abandonment and worthlessness, we would sway in the wind with no boundaries, operating from a place fearing that people would leave us. We have the great ability of changing like chameleons, always good at blending in and not making waves.

The lie was that people would love us and only stay if we were quiet and agreeable, catering to their needs and disregarding ourselves. It's a life of walking on eggshells and it can be dangerous by taking us down roads we wouldn't have gone down on our own; risking everything to feel loved.

The truth is that healthy Boundaries give us good foundations and they keep us safe, protecting our hearts, our feelings, emotions and personalities.

"A boundary is simply you telling someone else what you will be doing. It is the ability to communicate that you have priorities and a dedication to protect those priorities. - Danny Silk"

Chapter Nine
It's Just The Beginning

Now, my Healing Journey has come full circle. In April of 2017, I reunited with my family after 37 years. I worked through the pain, disappointment and released all resentments and anger and most of all, I truly forgave everyone. But, it wasn't enough to only have head knowledge, God wanted to see the action and what better way to demonstrate that, but to return home.

Understand, I did the work with the Lord; I changed and I was healed, but most of what I left behind remained the same. It was so empowering to return home and know that I conquered my fears and won. I finally felt that I was a mature heart-healed woman who came out the other side better than before.

I know that on my own I could never have accomplished any of what this book represents. Even writing it was a divine inspiration and a download from God. I am overwhelmed with emotion when I consider all of the times God has saved and protected me and I'm overjoyed at how much God loves me, all of me, every fiber in my body. Now, the *Little Girl of 3* is exactly where she is supposed to be.

The *Little Girl of 3* had no control over the family that she was born into. A family filled with hurt, pain, circumstances and situations beyond her control; with a belief that she was invisible and that no one cared. But, God had a different plan, He knew her before she was born, giving her a strong warrior spirit to carry her through the long journey.

God says to each and every woman reading this book: *"you are relevant, worthy, extraordinary, strong, able and delightfully beautiful and life giving."* The *Little Girl of 3* thrives now with the deeper meaning in her heart of life and love and her quest to get back to Eden.

One of her life long question was "where do I fit?" And the Father answered *"with me of course!"* Holding His hand, this *Little Girl of 3* isn't afraid anymore, and finally, she has the peace that surpasses all understanding, and knowing that this isn't the end, it's just The Beginning. ♡

"And the peace of God, which transcends all understanding, will guard your hearts and your minds in Christ Jesus."
Phil. 4:7

Conclusion
It's Time To Heal

It's time to give yourself permission to heal your heart and your emotional hurts.

It's time to break the cycles and the chains that bind and hold us captive in lies, deceptions, secrets, addictions, turmoil, hate and abuse.

It's time to live an unburdened life.

It's time for the captives to be set free and our eyes unveiled.

We have been wonderfully made for a time such as this and we need to be whole.

We need to take back all the pieces of our heart and heal.

It's time to live the life God has purposed for us. A life filled with Joy, Love, Abundance and Prosperity.

Today is the day to embark on the healing of your Heart. ♡

81

Bible Passages:

Psalms: 119:46: "*Then I'll tell the world what I find, speak out boldly in public, unembarrassed.*"

Psalms: 66:16: "*All believers, come here and listen, let me tell you what God did for me.*"

Deuteronomy 31:8: "*The Lord himself goes before you and will be with you; he will never leave you nor forsake you. Do not be afraid; do not be discouraged.*

Psalms 34:17: "*The righteous cry out, and the Lord hears them; he delivers them from all their troubles.*"

Mark 1:10: "*Immediately coming up out of the water, He saw the heavens opening, and the Spirit like a dove descending upon Him.*"

Matthew 10:16: "*Behold, I send you out as sheep in the midst of wolves; so be shrewd as serpents and innocent as doves.*"

Proverbs 26:11: "*Like a dog that returns to his vomit is a fool who repeats his folly.*"

Little Girl of 3

Matthew 18:22: *"Jesus answered, "I tell you, not seven times, but seventy-seven times."*

Philippians 4:7: *"And the peace of God, which transcends all understanding, will guard your hearts and your minds in Christ Jesus."*

THANK YOU!

To Everyone who has purchased, sponsored, or walked through your own journey of the "*Little Girl of 3*" and has read this book, I sincerely **Thank You**, and send Warm Virtual Hugs; I wholeheartedly appreciate you.

Feel free to connect with me and join forces, so we can ***Empower Other Women*** around the World; that they too can be healed, set free and delivered from all past pain and hurt inflicted when they were a *Little Girl of 3*. I invite you to connect with me on my social media platform by simply looking for "*Little Girl of 3.*"

My email is littlegirlof3@gmail.com. I look forward to connecting with each and every one of you. Shalom. ♡

Donna

www.ingramcontent.com/pod-product-compliance
Lightning Source LLC
LaVergne TN
LVHW021411080426
835508LV00020B/2562